Like A Butterfly

Copyright © 2022 Yeldā Ali

All rights reserved.

ISBN: #9798848535426

DEDICATION

To the ten teenage girls who wrote this anthology.

CONTENTS

War	Pg 1
Letters	Pg 7
Boundaries	Pg 17
Innocence	Pg 22
Love & Lie	Pg 29
About	Pg 38

FOREWORD
By Yeldā Ali

When I started working with the girls, we met every Thursday morning; I'd go on to brag about them to my friends and family until the following Wednesday evening. *They're so creative. You wouldn't believe what they did today. They are what it means to be authentic! They're so kind. They've seen so much. They inspire me. We made this incredible song today.* The list of things I would share goes on and on. Even so, I would still witness resistance and sometimes downright rejection while we took that journey. These girls have reasons to doubt and mistrust.

The illustration on the front cover of *Like A Butterfly* was made by a shy girl, who consistently and kindly refused to participate in class. I was less concerned about her attendance, and more interested in connecting with her. When Covid-19 restrictions finally let up and I was allowed to visit in person, she sat close to me and asked if I wanted to see some of her art. We eagerly and excitedly thumbed through her pieces together, and she answered questions I had about the process and inspiration behind her work. When I told her I wanted to incorporate 'Butterfly' as cover art (the symbolism!) for this anthology, her lips swung upwards ever so slightly, eyes sparkling as she nodded encouragingly.

The book's back cover, like most of the work in this anthology, came from prompts in class that we worked on. When I first prompted the girls to write about war, and what it meant to them outside of politics, two of my students ran off into a corner to seemingly play a game. As I watched them playfully argue, laugh loudly, and scribble on one sheet of paper together, I assumed they weren't participating, until they ran up to the computer screen and said, *Ms. Yeldā do you want to see what we made?* There were many games of Tic Tac Toe on the page, and I was blown away by the simplicity in their creativity. This was a constant: how creatively these girls express themselves.

Outside of prompts about courage, forgiveness, strength, and other topics we discussed, the girls submitted more personal entries from their prison journals. It took time to build this trust in class, and it was centered around remembering that these are not average students on Zoom in a pandemic. These are teenage prisoners who lack choice, safety, and freedom, doing the best they can with the world on their shoulders. There were days where class energy was minimal, unfocused, and frustrated. There were days where the energy was hopeful, vulnerable, and determined. Regardless of the day, I knew deeply that it was a class where the students were the teachers, and I was grateful to be in their school, learning about the full spectrum of humanity—from injustice to integrity.

WAR

Heart & Brain

People always say,
Think before you do.
Others say,
Follow your heart.

If I follow my heart,
I'll hurt the people closest to me.
If I follow my brain,
I'll hurt myself.

Dark

My skin is dark,
my mind is bright.
Scared driving at night,
pulled over at red lights.

2022, We still have to fight,
We, the opposite of white.
My people fought for fairness,
not no damn special awareness.

Put me in a dark room,
I'll be hard to find.
Bring me out in public,
I'll get the spotlight.
Nah it ain't right,
but fuck it—that's life.

Cops tell us back away,
guns aimed higher than the neckline.
Since we a darker shade,
they don't see us the same.
They claim we a threat,
so they play "afraid".

<u>When?</u>

War is when people or things are battling.
War is betrayal between two long term friends.
War is about drugs.
When is war over?

Strong, Beautiful, Smart Survivor

I found out you died and I don't know how to feel. My mind and heart are at war.

My heart hurts because you were the only father I knew for a long time and even though you're not my father, you definitely played the role and I thank you for doing so. You also made my mother happy and that is the best thing you've ever done.

My mind is telling me you got what you deserved because of what you did to me. But I forgive you, I forgive you, I forgive you. As much as I want to hate you, I can't bring myself to do it.

Because of you, I wouldn't be able to do half the things that I can now. Because of you, I refuse to play the victim role. Because of you, I am who I am. A strong, beautiful, smart survivor.

Thank you.

Like Paper

My body's like paper.
Instead of a pen, I use a razor.
Leaving ugly scars all over my skin.
To be exact, my arms.

LETTERS

Akeem

I love you the most, I try not to cry.
I love you for life, one hug for the last time.

January 9th was the day I got the call,
The call that broke my heart for good, for all.

I never got to say bye or kiss upon your head,
Six feet under is where God wanted you instead.

Even though you're only physically gone,
my heart feels dull like a winter without snow.

The Keem Keem to my Keke, my lil man for life.
If I have a do over, I'll go through it twice.

Not to sound shady or to sound rude,
God made his plans, not much I can do.

I love you the most, I try not to cry.
My dear little brother, this is goodbye.

Not bye to your soul, but bye to this boulder.
I blamed myself because I am older.

I love you the most, I try not to cry.
Dear Akeem, I'll see you in the next life.

Bright

You the only one who made me feel I had a purpose,
the one I wanted to be around cause I never felt worthless.

Every time I needed you, you gave me your shoulder to cry on.
I guess it's kinda sad to say, you were the only one I could rely on.

You always told me to not get caught up, but I did.
I should've told you how I felt, instead my feelings I hid.

Just the thought of you makes me smile, it breaks my heart that I won't see you for a while.
I still listen to our song, the one I used to cry to, on replay, don't forget how much I love you.

That will always remain the same.
The only one that showed me love, when all I felt was pain.

<u>Suave World</u>

I should've been by your side, but I left you all alone.
Swiped up on all your messages, I should've taken that trip back.

I didn't wanna believe it when she said you were gone.
I looked straight in her eyes and told her she was wrong.

It's your world, even when you're in the sky.
I love you Best Friend, fly high.

<u>Dear Mom Pt. 1</u>

I just wanted to tell you my life story!!

I've been raped 4 times by men you thought you loved. I've been abused and misused. I've been heartbroken so many times.

Do you really know me?

I have PTSD and it makes my hands shake. I really need some help Mom. I'm hurting and you don't see it. You were supposed to be there to watch me grow up but you let alcohol get in the way. I told you many times that you hurt me and you never questioned how.

You were never here. I've been raped, locked up, cheated on, back stabbed, lied to, kidnapped, almost trafficked, overdosed, struggled with mental health.

And you expect me to understand?

Dear Mom Pt. 2

The mom I once had was tall, dark, and caring.
The mom I have now, I have to beg to call or visit me.

I wish I had a normal family.
I wish I had a dad that went to work and would protect me.
I wish my mom picked me up from school, take me to the movies.
But for me, wishes never come true.

It always gets worse before it gets better, that's what my mom says.
I still don't know what the truth is.

Dear Mom Pt. 3

My mom has always lied to me. Starting with the easter bunny, all the way to the tooth fairy, just lie after lie. One day, she called me telling me that she was coming to visit and she never showed. You can't believe anything that comes out this woman's mouth.

But what can I do? She's the "parent".

Sometimes I feel that I'm more mature. Times I feel like I'm the parent, taking care of a grown ass lady. I'm only 14 and I helped pay the rent and phone bills. I would have to steal to help you buy drugs. Watch plenty of men come through our home just to abuse and misuse you. Yeah, it does hurt to see your mom drink her problems away, or smoke til she can't function properly.

I know how it feels for your mom not to respect you as a person, as if you don't matter. When my mental health got really bad, I started going to psych wards. Being prescribed to so many things, being moved to so many placements made me go insane.

But what can I do? I've been dealt a bad hand.

When grandpa died, I lost everything including myself. I started cutting, drinking, and smoking all at the age of 13. I didn't know what to do. I was lost and I couldn't find myself. I was hurting. I started acting out for people to notice but they never did.

Daddy's Girl

Daddy, I didn't have to kill you,
you were gone before I had the time.
When you left, I always thought every Black man I saw was you.
I had to get it through my head that you were gone.

I've always been scared of you but not anymore.
Not after you tore my itty bitty heart in two.
I thought I could always have hope in you but you let me down.
I was 11 when they took you, why couldn't you stay huh?

Why did you have to do what you did?
I wish we could get through this.
But you never call me, you never think about me.
Guess what? I think about you, you know I do.

This can't be fixed, it just can't.
I waited for too long, it's time to let go and move on.
I'm sorry, see you in another lifetime.
Love you pops.

<u>Pretty Girl</u>

Hi Katie, I miss you so much and I wish you were still here. I could really use someone to talk to. Life is hard right now. I can barely see mom and dad, and a whole bunch of other stuff.

I know you're watching over me all the time because I can feel your presence every day. You're always on my mind. Every single day. I feel like I actually know if you were still here I'd be different.

Mom said she's going to see you soon and I really wish I was going with her because I have so much to tell you.

I'm almost 18 now. I know, it's crazy right? These past 12 years without you have been so hard. You weren't just my cousin, you were my sister and best friend. I know I was young but I remember that day like it was yesterday.

And I know you're up there, pain-free, no longer suffering from anything. And having the time of your life. I also know you're the one who answers my prayers a lot of the time and I thank you for that.

Miss you unconditionally, forever and always. Rest easy pretty girl.

Dear Past Me

You should've respected yourself more, fought less, cared more. You should've been more alert, in choosing your friends, and boyfriends. If only you cared more about your health, instead of caring about your next high, you may have saved some of the relationships you lost.

A year ago, I was told, *you only care about yourself.* I didn't believe it then, but now I see that they were right about you, past self. I can't believe someone can be so self-centered. Stealing your parents hard-earned money, leaving expensive rehab, well guess what?

I'll never let me be like you again.

BOUNDARIES

My Space

I really need my space,
today is not my day.
Can you please back away?
I am not okay.

When I feel surrounded
my mind gets clouded.
No other way around it,
I need my space.

I am not okay,
I beg you to stay away.
Your actions are to blame,
you need to learn your frame.

I set my boundaries,
please respect them.
How dare you disrespect them?
I said no, you are not welcome.

My space,
my space,
my space,
my space.

Success

Need to know your place,
and stay away
is how it's bound to be,

I just need my space,
need some time to
set some boundaries.

I need to set some goals,
just to be aware,
just to be proud of me.

A lot of hate,
just concentrate
cause people be doubting me.

I love and hate,
I play my role like you,
I don't discriminate.

Don't mean to scare,
I know I'm stepping hard,
don't feel intimidate.

Caged Heart

My heart was once free like a bird.
It's now locked up and hard to reach,
that's how I keep my heart.

I'm scared to get hurt so I stay in protective mode.
Being hurt hurts really bad.

Love or Lust?

I love the way you overstep my boundaries and make my body feel.
I love the way you also make sure I'm okay and safe.

So I ask myself, am I love or lust?
Not only does my body crave your touch, my heart craves your connection.

INNOCENCE

Unforgiving Soul

Sometimes when I'm alone, I cry because I'm all I got.
The tears I cry are warm, they flow with life and take no form.
I cry because my heart is torn, and I find it difficult to carry on.

If I had an ear to confide in, I would cry amongst treasured friends.
Who do you know that takes time to care?
The world moves fast and would rather pass me by then to stop and figure out what made me cry.

Come Back To Me

Pretty smiles, deceiving laughs, and people who
dream with their eyes open.
Lonely children, unanswered cries, and souls who
have given up on hope.

Fairy tales that never come true break hearts too,
and selfish people who lie to me Dad, selfish people like you.

Sidewalk Pt. 1

I just wanted to be a kid, grow up at my own pace.
It's kinda hard to achieve, in the streets with a pretty face.

You can walk down the street when a cat decides to call you,
you walk over, see what he wants, that's when he know he gotchu.

He said, *forget ya whole past, I'ma give you the whole world.*
You didn't think he'd do things that'd traumatize a little girl.

You let him beat on you all the time cause you knew you had no choice, you knew it'd get even worse if you chose to use your voice.

You let him take advantage of you, knowing it'd only cause you pain.
It got even worse when he offered you money to fuck with the whole gang.

He got you hooked on drugs to eliminate any feeling of regret,
this was only the beginning of your journey, *how much worse can it get?*

Petals

I remember when I was innocent,
not a care in the world.
When I look in the mirror,
I can't find that little girl.
She stares right back at me,
but doesn't speak a word.
Her lips move and she begins to cry,
no sounds can be heard.

She points to my arm.
I reveal scars that relieved me of my madness.
Remembering the relief it brought my body,
as I scarred my body with all my sadness.
The walls close in around me,
and my demons scream louder.
In a world full of pain,
I tend to cry.

They call me
the weeping flower.

Questions

Do you feel angry?
When you get hurt, are you mad?
Or do you feel hatred?

It's hard to feel good feelings,
when you are so sad.

Bad Kid

I was always the "bad kid"
that's why they labeled me as.
People told me that I was crazy
because I didn't know how to act.
Imagine your family disowning you
for your mental health issues.
I don't have to imagine,
that's what I went through.

LOVE & LIE

Healing, Not Healed

Though it's a not-so-pretty journey, it's a beautiful outcome.
It can be as easy as accepting something and coming to terms with it. It can be as hard as letting a loved one go.

Though healing may look different, it can feel similar. Like getting over a breakup, or accepting the death of a loved one. In both scenarios, you have to say goodbye to someone you care for. In both scenarios, you need healing.

I lost one of my close friends to a drug overdose, I went through a lot of feelings. The biggest and most life-changing experience was healing.

I went from blaming myself and hating the world, to accepting the loss. I went from not leaving my bed, to trying my best to live my life.

That's what she always told me to do. A part of healing is having these bad days, which I still have. I may never be healed but I'll forever be healing.

Her!

Honor thy mother and thy father they say.
Where does it say abandon your child and walk away?

For a man with five kids, prior to the sixth,
you walked out on your child like she didn't exist.
Now, for a woman with only one child, you allowed yourself
to get handcuffed and put away for awhile.

Leaving her child with a man who did nothing
but drink, sipping on rolling rock and doing his thing.
Growing up, that little girl
met a lot of females trying to play the mother role.

Cynthia, Allison, Roxie, and Megan,
yet none of those names were called in trial.
That child couldn't even recognize her birth giver,
yeah that took awhile.

I Wish

My head is spinning, boy you got me trippin,
thinking it was finna be you from the beginning.
Now you got me wishing.

I wish I neva caught no feelings, I wish we neva had no dealings.
I wish, I wish, I wish.
I wish that you was true to your word, and held me down like a man should.
I wish, I wish, I wish.

See everything we wish for, we don't get.
Love I had for you was too strong, now I feel regret.
You had it all, you settled for less,
you hitting rock bottom, would've given my best.
And part of growing up is to forgive,
but best believe the lies will relive.

I wish I neva caught no feelings, I wish we neva had no dealings.
I wish, I wish, I wish.
I wish that you was true to your word, and held me down like a man should.
I wish, I wish, I wish.

You had me going crazy, fucked my head up.
Overreacting, had me thinking I was messed up.

Every day we getting into it,
every otha day you act clueless.
Now you got me feeling so ruthless,
lying but I know what the truth is.

I wish I neva caught no feelings, I wish we neva had no dealings.
I wish, I wish, I wish.
I wish that you was true to your word, and held me down like a man should.
I wish, I wish, I wish.

Lies Pt. 1

You said you loved me,
why'd you lie?
Why'd you let me gain butterflies,
then let them fly?
All the memories we made,
you based the roots on lies.
You allowed me to try,
over a million times.

How could you waste my time?
Why would you take what was mines?
You made me go insane,
like I was losing my brain.
It's you I blame,
but then again that's on me.
I was living a dream,
a fairytale that's beyond me.

Yes I am hurt,
but the lesson has been learned.
I will forgive, I won't forget,
there is nothing I regret.

Lies Pt. 2

What I know now, I wouldn't have allowed myself to sink.
Sink in these drinks, that's all it takes.
That's all it took for me to be hooked, for me to get booked.
You let us go, you you let us down, you let me go, you let me down.
Most important—you lied!

Regrets

Every time I was with you, I didn't wanna say goodbye.
Even the thought of losing you, made me wanna cry.
I really loved you, and I thought you loved me too.
Even when your hands were around my throat, making me turn blue.

I told you I wanted a kid, you told me you were with it.
Then you pushed me down the stairs, and told me it was to kill it.

I laid in your arms, and felt safe and not alone.
Every time I went to leave, you said I can't go home.
I still think about you, especially when I cry.
Cause you were the one to make me feel like it was my time to die.

No Love

I've been looking for some love (love, love)
Try to play me, you a dub (dub, dub)
I've been throwing this, it's enough (nuff, nuff)
Baby why you giving up (up, up)

Hold me up, don't slow me down (down, down)
When I need, you not around (round, round)
You just kept letting me down (down, down)
You was nowhere to be found (ound, ound)

You was my baby through the storm,
that's why I fucked with you.
You had me thinking we would make it
but it wasn't true.

We in the dark, I shined a light
so I can see it through,
You had me thinking it was us
but it was really you.

You played me,
are you crazy?
It was sunny, now it's rainy, on a daily
Baby why you acting shady, you so shady

Value

What is love to you?
What is love with no value?
When you mess with him,
do you feel the love in you?

ABOUT *LIKE A BUTTERFLY*

Literacy for Incarcerated Teens (LIT) is a non-profit organization ending illiteracy among New York's incarcerated young people by inspiring them to read.

2012: **Robert Galinsky**, artist and educator, partners with LIT to bring teenagers in prisons and jails to access more films, books, music, theater, and live guest artists.

2021: Galinsky invites **Yeldā Ali**, storyteller and women's safety advocate, for author Q&A. After meeting and immediately connecting with the girls, Yeldā becomes a weekly creative writing and poetry facilitator.

2022: Ali leads incarcerated students through ten dedicated weeks of writing, drawing, dancing, and singing to produce their first published collection: *Like A Butterfly*.

—

Special Thanks To: Robert Galinsky, Karlan Sick, Mary Elizabeth Wendt, Dana Lehrman, Judy Frost, Elizabeth Dreier, Judith Karpatkin, Gigi Blanchard, Marybeth Zemen, Jessica Fenster-Sparber, Karen Surgeary, and Susan Ginter.